Whose broken is this?

Also by John Passant and published by Ginninderra Press
Songs for the Band Unformed

John Passant

Whose broken is this?

Whose broken is this?
ISBN 978 1 76041 635 5
Copyright © text John Passant 2018

First published 2018 by
GINNINDERRA PRESS
PO Box 3461 Port Adelaide 5015 Australia
www.ginninderrapress.com.au

Contents

Introduction	7
Caught between	9
Our reading room is closed	12
Bigly bombs	14
Old school memories	15
Fragments from a Gasoline Pony afternoon	16
The falling leaf	18
Understanding	20
There is no time, any more	21
For a friend	23
So they tell us	24
The spreaders and their plagues	26
She rises the moon	28
The beach walk	33
Ringing home	35
Of nothing, for nothing	36
The breath of tomorrow is yours	37
What time is this?	39
Where flowers their freedom	40
To help my daughter	43
I was reading Brecht today	44
Our home	45
The beach is near	46
Farewell young man	47
Why?	49
The politics of alone	50
Whose broken is this?	52
The friend returns	54
In the beginning was the end	55
On being unfree	56

The poem in my head is dead	58
We must wear a poppy	60
The dead do not smile	62
The poetry of tax	66
Unread	70
Morning comes early	71
For a friend, again	73
On the sewer we sup	75
The cricket crowd	76
Do not play cricket with my soul	78
Farewell, old man	80
Citizen	82
Open libraries	83
These broken waters of the truth	84
Come, join our cause	86
We hear your thunders	89
In the grave of no	91
Lenin's anvil is worn	93
I can no more	95
Monday is the time of silence	98
Who carries the carrion?	99
Where are our words, today?	101
October is coming	102
Still free	104
To a tree	106
The butcher reigns	108
The once a year of cheer	109
Sing with me in the rain	114
Waiting for May	116

Introduction

This is my second volume of poetry published by the wonderful people at Ginninderra Press. It follows the first, *Songs for the Band Unformed*, in that it deals with the political and the personal, sometimes together, sometimes separately.

However, as I hope *Whose broken is this?* shows, the division between the political and the personal is an artificial one. As one slogan of the 1960s pointed out, the personal is political, and the political is personal.

We live in a deeply fractured world, one where we are the broken. We shape the system every day. We build it every day. And every day it repays us with alienation, exploitation and oppression. But amid that despair it is clear too that we are the hope, the solution.

In among those shadows are the bright lights of family and friends, of lovers and leavers who remind us every day that the human still exists, and that we are it.

My thanks again to my children, Michael and Louise, and to Patricia, always Patricia.

In memory of my father, Joe.

John Passant, 2018

Caught between

Hope and realism collide
Depression rises, and subsides,
The individual in the honeycomb
We drone, they throne

We of the community battle,
Outside, inside, all sides
Their river is wide
Our boat is small

And the rowing tires
Me, and the crew
Their water destroys our fires
Mine, anew

Anew, that is it
The drowned man rises
And with him all the others
The crowd on the bank cheers

We are home, not alone
But in the grasp of being
The cusp of becoming
If our boat does not sink

Is it sturdy?
Does it leak?
These are the questions
Of our weakness

And then the bleakness descends
Sometimes the returning friend
Almost, for we cannot
Resurrect ourselves

The waters are too deep
The enemy does not sleep
And in the system's insomnia
Our dreams cry, afar, too far

The dead do not dream
Nor the living, in reality
All is at it seems
Their ageing, our frailty

But still we row
For the future must begin
Here and now
We are atow

And still the dark clouds
Rise and thunder
Loud before us
They sing their chorus

The rowing has stopped
No anchor dropped
In safe harbours
We bob on their waves

No Christ to save us
But ourselves
I see you on the shore
I hope to be there

Before, before what?
Nothing, it was a fleeting thought
And dead men do not think
Nor the living, in truth

There is no boat, no river, no shore
No cheering crowds to greet us
All but the storm
Will they beat us

And I, myself?
I cannot tell
Caught between
Our heaven, their hell

Our reading room is closed

Poets talk too much
And not enough
In a language that is tough
And not so brusque

That is all we do
Talk, or not,
Unread,
Unless we rent the TS room

No one reads the prophets
In the time of madness
We are not seers
In a world of sadness

Our Reading Room is closed
Our Library has no books
And the man who lived there
Has died

There are other rooms
And words do write
Alone, together
The image is of never

And the scratchings grow
While the armies of the ignorant
Know everything
And gather for their war

There is no more
Only more, and more
Ginger up the troops
Finger up the loops

To total, all total
The end, the end
If we let them
Will we?

Or send their hell to hell
That is our task
I ask not much
But the sweet touch

Of peace, and freedom
Of democracy and justice
Do not despair as I do
Join us

And in the joining
End this misery
And in the joining
Unite, be free

Bigly bombs

They are the best
Not chemicals
Just a bomb
Of all destruction

The dead are not worthy
Women, children and old men
Who cares?
Who dares?

Winsome, dressed in black
Takes the stage
And looking back
Laughs in rage

And we shake our heads
Inside, outside
Dead, all dead
Them, and us

In God we trust
And other lies
Their God or yours?
Not mine

What God could give us this?
What have I missed?
The bigly bomb comes too
It waits for me, and you.

Old school memories

I went past my old school today
Saint John Vianney is its name
On that first day
59 years ago,
I ran away
I should have kept going

I remember the beatings, of others mainly
The angry nuns, the shouting
The fear of God,
Beaten in, always beaten in
With stories and the rod

I remember the football exploits
The athletics
My proud achievements
But not the reading, the writing
The numbers that I learnt
Times tables drummed in
Like everything
It hurt

I went past my old school today
I did not look at it
I looked ahead
And kept going
I fled
My memories destroyed me
The boy is dead

Fragments from a Gasoline Pony afternoon

The light is cold
Crawling cross the old across
Of hearts

The night is bold
It fits, it starts
And rising places wisely
Hell in heaven

None are forgiven
Where the sun is gone
Frozen time
Takes it toll
There is no rhyme
In the hole of black, day

Except the music
The music plays its fingertips
Through the mind of man
And the women, always the women
Hug the notes
And understand
The band begins

To tune, that is the question
And on reflection
There is none
Only fun
The fun that runs its coarse
Fingers through our hair
There is nowhere but here
To live, to survive

In the loop of swinging notes
From high to low
Watch them grow
Their tentacles strive, alive

Our hive of living, love
There is nothing else
But self
In others
Being us

The falling leaf

It is May Day
There are no workers
Marching past
An old man sits next to me
My old man
Waiting, at last
To be free

This is your freedom, Dad
It lives here now
This is your freedom, Dad
It lives in you now
It is you
You know how

Let us walk quietly
And look for things lost
Today and yesterday
That is my choice
It is yours too
At least for the moment

And the sleeping
That has you
Catches me too
Afternoons snore
Beyond your shores
Onto my island

My rich land
Of no money
But love
That falling leaf
From your tree
That is you
That is me

Let the goodbye wait
For another year
Let the wakings arrive
For both of us
In this we meet
Our humanity

Where mine is yours
Mine is what you gave me
And all I can do,
I hand you your past
Today,
For tomorrow
And each day after

Then we joke
Your laughter is mine
I don't understand
But I do,
This journey is me
This journey is you

Understanding

I do not understand Marx
In all his volumes
I do not understand Hegel
Apparently
Lukacs loses me
Totally some might say

And yet I know the struggle
Class against class
Them and us
The value that is exploitation

Enough of sly references!
Our side is my essence
A man of emotions,
Of guesses at life
Watering the strife
To negate the hate
And blossom the love

I can read
And begin to understand
But I can feel
And in that I am woman
And I am man
I am me, I am you
And then I understand

There is no time, any more

We walk through the forest
Of grey hair
To the minute hands
Of time

We talk through
The wood
Of wobbly knees
To the Beltanes
Of mine

And in doing that
Recall
The May Days
Marching past

When we strode, stiff-backed,
Slick-haired au naturel,
To the prisons
Of our heaven
And the freedom
Of our hell

Our parades are faded
Skin memories taken
Live signs jaded
The road awakens
For the lonely passerby
Who sees the past
With eyes today

Pausing alone,
Not seeing us
Or them
Real,
The ghosts are
Past time

She drops the red rose
In memory of other times
For now she sees
My life, our crimes
Of justice,
Thought
But never won

The road is striven
The driver driven
To the end
That never ends
Nor finds its way
Except to where we were

The clock strikes midnight
And stops
The second hand is wound
Back and put down
Silent in its sound
There is no time
Any more

For a friend

I do not know you
But I do
My friend
On this book
We talk, and laugh
You know me
And the eternal
The sadness that is
Has taken you
It shakes me too
These fake days
Celebrate the moneyed ways
And make the good cry
We know why
I am with you
From afar
And in words

So they tell us

The bugle calls
And the young men answer
Marching, marching
There is no dancer
But the bullet-fire disco
While the warmth that radiates
From above,
Bellows its name
Into the flames of love
Or so they tell us

Everything is love
The blood, the bones
The time that crawls
Past dead thrones
And clutches hope
Dying in the clasp
Grasping life askew
Nothing old, all anew
Or so they tell us

Christmas has gone
Our songs are buried
Next to their dead
The same look
A parting shot
No romance
Nothing hot
In that glance
Or so they tell us

Four years later
The trenches empty their coprolites
The bowels of heaven
End in workers' guns
No return to the old days
The old ways are gone
Hurried along
The new song will uplift
Or so they tell us

But the tune remains
The same blood,
The same young men
A decade apart
Gather again
To restart the dance of death
And we do,
For so they tell us

The spreaders and their plagues

The dead diseases return
Their crippling arms raised
To salute the golden dawn
Do we forget the agony?
The iron lung of hunger?
The cry of the six million?

Some do
With different words
Intent is samed
It remains, disguised
In other flames
The doctors die
No one is,
All led beyond
The done

And in the doing
Become ourselves
In overcoming
The others
Denied their freedom
We are freed, we think
We breathe,
They do not
Is that it?
Why, again and again
This same, old shit?

It is in the bones,
The DNA, of the way
We produce
There is no use for it
Seize the day
Kill the old ways
While we are few
We remain the many
In the pool
Of the unknown
Swimming tided
With and against

We will scale
Not just the fence
But Chomolungma itself
And rid the world
Of the spreaders
And their plagues
Not in The Hague
But by ourselves
Not alone
But together
Forever

She rises the moon

Every month God bleeds
His needs, unmanned
Her deeds, at hand
The intersex of love
Is caught,
Between the two

This She knew
And wild walked the side
Until His feet bled,
Well, heeled

Between the end
And the felt
Stood potential
Drained to gain
Renewed the fame
Again, and again

She rises the moon
And sups her song
Of hymn
The twin dances
Our double helix
Together, apart

Art is dead
Gender ends
To become one
The one, the all
Batter down the richest door

Mateship sailed, soiled,
The myth of men,
Of outback fuckers
In a world of cities
And out-of-luckers

The equality of fools
Of shared nothing
The solidarity of tools
Honed on the loneliness
Of space

The great white plains
That exist in heads alone
Explain too much
And so cannot be
Explained

Howard's beggars
Line their streets
The neat array
Of destitutes
Denied a life
For profits call
A shadowed hope
A tortured fall

The armied stand,
Old, hand in hand
No one helps
No one cares
They take their place
They part their hair
Of what remains
With brylcreem smiles
And fevered air

Memories of the dead
Arise
Like ghosts
Before their only eye
Both them and us
There are two sides
Coffined
In the living bog
Of war

The sick man walks
The doctors' street
Row upon row
Very neat
But he cannot enter
The houses closed
Only the propertied may pose
For deeper images

The battered woman
Kids akimbo
Searches, shelter-skeltered,
And broken limbed, for home
The empty are full
The full emptied
By government largesse
The gutter her mattress

The embers die
The black woman cries
She remembers
The world without
The white man
The doubt gone
Disease and suicide
And poverty
Spiritual, material
Have blossomed
On the land that is not hers
Any more

In camps far away
Concentrated behind
The blinds of openness
Are those who sought help
Thrown from the good boat mateship
Like all the others

The kings and queens
Of mates
Rule us
The rich men and women
Hate us
The crippled, the poor, the black
The women in the back

Their loudspeakers blast
Fairness and freedom
We rotten away
Caught in the sway
Of their money
And their power

Come rise,
Rise against
And for
Against them, for us
For freedom from and freedom for
Let's batter down
Their richest door
And give their gold
To us, the poor

The beach walk

The seashore sings your name
I hear it as I walk
As we used to walk
Along the beach
Not long ago

I remember the salt smell
The wind gentle in its telling
And your stride slowing
As you said hello to those
You did not know

Your smile leapt to them
Then swept back again
And captured the terrain
Of dogs on leashes
And babies in prams
Led by owners
Or parents

The sun smiled
And saw all was good
And you knew
You talked to me of futures
Without you
You knew
The sun would not smile
One day

And yet, it does
For me
Because of you
And for you,
Because of me,
In memory and memoriam
Of love,
And thanks, old man

Ringing home

I caught myself thinking
I should call you
To remind you
The football was on
Your phone is cancelled
As are you
The dead line of life
You don't answer any more
The football is on
No words exchange
I watch alone

Of nothing, for nothing

What if the voice loses?
And the sound departs,
Runs its way
No words, just play
Time to reflect,
Inside is hiding, hidden
Thoughts unbidden
Unsaid
Taken from the silence
Its head
Written, nothing
It cannot be
Can it?

The line remains the same
The same
Over and over again
The word of no word
The noise of no noise
Hounded from the truth
Of no truth
Other than the writing
That is nothing
Of nothing
For nothing

The breath of tomorrow is yours

I stand with the illusionists
And those who have illusions
Well, those card men and women
Who trick us to waste two dollars
To survive
Not two billion to thrive

And the illusioned?
What do we say to them?
That two dollar card games are tricks?
They know this reality
Then how do we explain
That the two billion is the real game?

History's ways wend
Like a river of slow bends
Toxic, full of waste
Upstream, the fresh water floods
Rushing to rid the past
Of filth
In haste we rebuild
Tomorrow, today
And then the card sharks
Show their truth
Their arms built strong
Their tongues sleek
And full of El Dorado
We are not weak
We are the torrent
That seeks and sends
The ends to build the new

To drive the money lenders
And all the motley, their crew
To the bottom
Of their river

Their solid melts
The disillusion has died
As the illusions ride
To join the illusioned
In fantasy writ real
Live, love, feel
The day approaches
Silent, steady here, rushing there
And we can broach
The socialism of care
The breath of tomorrow is yours
Illusioned no more

What time is this?

There is no call in the land of phones
Only places to hide alone
Where every step captures the past
Knowing forever it cannot last
There is no shining in the land of sun
Only wandering to avoid its gun
Where every shot repeats the now
Knowing forever that is the how

There is no rain in the land of clouds
Only permission granted aloud
Where every shadow paints the near
Knowing forever is always the fear

There is no ice in the land of cold
Only the young growing old
Where every day is our tomorrow
Knowing forever this perfect sorrow

Where flowers their freedom

I saw their ghosts today
In something that I read
I feel their ghosts forever
In something that they said
And they say now, and yesterday
For all around is past

These ghosts are true,
They flourish in our land
Of reality as image, hand in hand
Where mirage dresses
Itself as truth
And black skins shine
In our white light
And rough-hewn plough
The darkness of their night

The black remains all day,
Friendless for us, and them,
Now and then, in every way
Here stands the rotting tree
In full bloom, that is the doom

Where flowers others' freedom, their liberty
Which rings its bell of death
And in a silent breath, of wisdom,
The wisdom that destroys,
Makes anew, all anew
For the few

And leaves us blackened in the sun
Whose days have come
To this burnt land
In rays of rage
We understand
But do not
Their lot is ours
Their pain is all
Their loss the fall
Of our humanity

Without power, we are all
The blackened faces of a past
That survives and still lasts
Today the same,
A way, no shame
As their shiny cars
Snake our streets
To places where the fancy eat
And make our money
On land that is not theirs
Who cares?

We do, the children of the dispossessed
The system of the prophets, blessed
With coins and turgid talk
We walk their mile
And do not smile
To make them rich
All rich

We are black, we are white
The toast of yesterday
On the breakfast of these kings
And queens
All is not what it seems

We must fight
Always fight,
White is black
We share what we lack
And in unison shout
Enough, get out

But they do not go
They stay, all stay,
This is their land now, they say
An old man in a boat made it so
And the sale of labour
Safe harbours favour
And the rich

Let's end their shouting
And drive them out
To bring to life, to live
All that we have
All that we give
All that we are, together.

To help my daughter

A daughter crying so far, far,
Away I fly will I, to her?
To rest my shoulder for her head
And hug her till it disappears
The fears, the hurt of life, and its end,
But it will not end
Like it has for her friend
Those tears of yours I hear
On the end of a phone
You are not alone
And I cry as well
Inside I too have died
We are not hell
We are alive, all alive
We live, love, life
And in the shadow of her death
Your life takes another breath
And I will be there soon
To help you, my daughter

I was reading Brecht today

I was reading Brecht today
Not in any normal way
There is no normal with Bertolt
Except the normal gestalt
Of a rational society
To come
Which means our eyes sometimes meet
And his words greet me
Down the paths of time
Without rhyme
Just truth
What to do?
You should read him too

Our home

Our home is destroyed, utterly destroyed
The home we built together over the years
With our friends, relatives and tears
The children trashed it in fake outrage
I have begun again to build another
Will you join me as I age?

The beach is near

The important thing is
To walk along the beach
And talk of Marx, and profit rates
And if we can
Grasp the time and state,
Within our reach
Or think, past rhyme and scan?

The hour to dance has come
We are the people
We are the one,
While the prammed mums
Push their kids
And women in bikinis
Show the sun their skin

The waves roll, eternal in,
The riders fraternal in their waves
We see the ballet of the water
And take sides, all curls
In this world,
That is the beach

Farewell young man

In the blacklight dark
That is my country
White men suit
Themselves to rule
Shining in their world
Of fading fools
While young boys lie
Hooded in our prisons
And boys on bikes die
From driving knife hands
No one asks why
They 'understand'

To question
Is sedition
To protest, riot
How dare you!
Keep quiet!
And the blue boys and girls
Take turns with twirls
Of pepper spray
To restore the order
Of the invaders

They waded ashore
Took it all
Took more
And left the dead,
Yesterday,
In our head
And left the dead,

Today, on the road
Mowed down
For being brown

This cannot change
It will not change
Until the white hearts
Are beaten
From their suits
Join us
In the streets of work
We will fight this hell
Until we well
The future for ourselves
Until we do, farewell
Farewell, all and everything

Farewell young man
Whose stolen land
The white man commands
The only way is this demand
It is our land

Why?

It is not the dark that threatens
But the light
It is midnight morning time
That gathers reason beyond imagination
That rides the train to backwardness
We must all fear

And in that journey we cannot see
The place is past and the world runs round
Where other people walk their lives
Leashed thinking unbound
Till the smell of others catches sight
And in our passage we praise the night

So join the queue of washing up
Of gentle people and genteel cups
Of tea and twitters
And anything that sets the beast astray
To find its way home far too soon
Where lives the yellow place,

The sky, the moon and face the truth
Shrouded in the blanket lies
Catch caught among the football joys
The noise abates and waits
Curled cute upon the traps
Sat awry until the mats begin
Their cry
Why?

The politics of alone

Alone, again,
Few comrades, and no friends
Alone, again, reading Marx
Between the darkness and the dark

Is this our Facebook life?
Entangled spaces wrapped in strife
Debate becomes our hate
And nothing, but nothing, awaits

The nihilism of words
Grasps the meaning of absurd
And free among the fields
Yields, all yields

Outside is cold,
I am old, and weary
The streets are full, dreary
People pass

Unheard, unseen
No in-between but silent
Still quiet, all quiet
On that front

We stand on corners
Shoehorners of the few
Panhandlers of the past
That might become the new

The magazine remains
The crowd unread
The parting waters divide
Us each again

While insults inflame
The dead in Mosul
And Aleppo cry
Why, oh why?

Whose broken is this?

Whose broken is this
The missing kiss
The mourning betrayal
The failure, failed
The catching light
That breaks, the night?
It is ours
In the hours between time
In the words before rhyme
In the place that was mine
And yours, the cause no doubt
Of agony beyond, beyond what?
The limit, the human, the forgotten
The true man, and woman, rotten
On the vine of life
Always woman, always wife
Arise the female, free
Take arms against the sea
Transcend, that is the end
And in the ending is the truth
Ruthless, vicious, violent
Welcome to our world
Where gathered rosebuds
From the graves
Of the saved, always saved,
Die in the reality of light
Sunlight, scoured
Empowered, to be weak
Turn our cheeks
The weekly thrashing is upon us

We cuss, and accept
The bloodied strap
The fondled nap of necked old men
When will this stop, again?
The sun is risen
The prison retreats
To the back of streets
More known
We are home
Where alone is
And the kids laugh
Their bath cleans
Mean streets
Mean nothing
I hear goodbyes
The cries and whys
They are mine
Always mine
Always, all ways
Such are my days
And nights
Caught between the passion
And the fright
Goodbye, good night

The friend returns

The friend returns
The eternal yearn
Of yearning made complete
Sweet success surrounds my feet
The feat that is defeat
This is the crossing
The turn that crosses all
The beginning and the fall
There is no other
Just the memory of mother
And places past
That did not last
But grasped the mind
Too kind, too kind,
We nod, agreed
I nod, not freed
But slaved again
In fakes of fame
Unknown, alone
The game remains
And in its wilting
The body lilting
Caught, not tilting,
Until the door behind
Opens in its way
And makes the end the stay
Forever

In the beginning was the end

I do not remember the wilderness
Nor the chill of its night
I do not remember the children
Nor the will of their fight

But I wandered in it, round and round
Never leaving, always found
And in the lies of their land
Began a journey to understand

In the beginning was the end
A whimpered bang among friends
For we are the wrong whose fight is right
We are the wronged in this ending light

We are the ones gathered and grown
We are the mightyless, alone
And in that garden, mown and neat
We fortune fame, not defeat

The harrowed hunger arrives
Behind our door
The children cry,
There is no more

And all the time the rhyme goes wrong
The ancient singer sings her song
While we sit deaf in our seats
Drinking the pleasure of our conceits

Tomorrow we march in columns and rows
We have escaped the eternal blows
Until the battle begins again
All is won, my ageing friend.

On being unfree

We live in the world of their bombs
The armed panopticon eyes us all
Kills the small, the poor, the fallen
For what, the prophet asks
There are no tasks but profit
All profit
Bow before its power
At the altar of the last
Remember no past
And gather guns that run the rind of time
There is no wine to drink away
Today, and tomorrow
Our worry, their sorrow
The bombs reign
Drones dominate
There is no refuge
From this hate
And so we start the heart, past heart
Caught between love
And the fate that awaits
The limbs, separated

The people, liberated
Stand silent
As slaughter untold
Unfolds, violent
Not quiet, not quite
Alone, alone
There is no love
Only bombs
The missiles of aplomb

Our power is the hour
Of their death
Nothing left
But the fleeing of the seeing
They know
On death's row
No life is belied
Only money, well thieved
And so ends
Their legless walk
Their tongueless talk
Their eyeless gaze

All of us, razed
To the ground
All found
All lost

There is no cost
But our lives
Our lives count
Their lives challenge
Not our bombs
But our humanity
They are bombed
We are unfree

The poem in my head is dead

We walked, old Ted and I
Along young Sally's run
Where the kangaroos' footprints,
Made mud, caught me, alone
The dog did but atone

His nose made rush
To yesterday's meals
This is how it feels
The freedom of four legs
Where no one begs

Except the men and women
The unforgiven
Whose story radios my ears
Their fears echo my mind
Ted walks behind

And having sniffed again
The weeds will bloom
Given room and his additions
I hear submissions
To walk this way

But I cannot knee today
Perhaps another way
Of gentle inclines
Will sway directions
In indiscretions of his or mine

It takes our time
Magpie silence, quiet ducks
You thought a rhyme?
Who gives a fuck?
I lost the thread

The poem in my head
Is dead
No notes accumulate
With dogs around
Sweet joy abounds

We must wear a poppy

We must wear a poppy
Today
That is the new way
Of freedom, evidently
Where men and women died
For that lie
And the rich victors
Retain their property
To spread their wealth
Footnoted democracy
And freedom

We join in
To beat them,
The enemy, just like us
Hard working
In God we trust
And our leaders
We are their bleeders
The bled, the maimed
The dead (of our side of course)

We worship a man
With a horse
A pacifist,
Wobbly against war
The whore of the system,
Broken, bespoken,
It fits amid the mud and blood
Of profits' shore

We cry, no more,
The soldiers rebel
Send the generals
To their hell
And the warmongers to perfidy
We cannot be free
In their chains

Our aims must be
New, a new society
Where war is memory
For its past
Not the last but one
But none
None at all

Join before we fall
To the khaki call
Of rich men past and present
Intent on our descent
Into the fields of death
Where poppies die
And lie amid the ruins
Ruined,

Like young men with arms
Killing young men with arms
Presented as charms
What sick society is this?
Give it the kiss
Of death.

The dead do not smile

The dead do not smile
They cannot laugh
And all the while
The red, white and blue
Takes a different hue
In the land of the stolen
Rotten, beholden to another cause
Our wars

Their wars are here
My tears fill the stadium
To welcome back our enemy
Where spent radium is free
And savagery unearths desire
That old revenge is higher than before
More and more is what we need

Their children bleed alone
In strongholds
Of those we do not understand,
For them no hand is outstretched
They are the wretched of our civilising
Cursed by the bombs of our denying
Flying overhead in the dead,
Of night,
Where might is right
There children cry
No one asks why

And the men, still men, of terror,
In suits or masks
Despise their mirrors
Through which they ask
Is Alice me
Or the Red King of the end
Where no dreams arise
Only ended lives, beneath the rubble
Of civilisation?

From the nations of liberty
Where none are free
Equality
Where none are equal
(Except in poverty)
And fraternity, of dog eat dog,
Barks its market
And raids the world
Curled in the coffin of liberation
These are our nations

Besuited armoured states
Denuded humanity awaits
On both sides rides the train
Of death alone for unpain
Amid moments where a minutes' gain
Is immortalised
And stains our memory forever
This is the never of the past

Made fast, alive in today's terror
We are the mistake
They are the error

Leaders, never, wrong
The story short
The tale long
Where go these grave words?
To the valley of the unheard
Who cannot now rise up

We can, that is the hope
For love,
The child of peace
Is our want
Not war or slaughter
Of sons and daughters
We do not know

We can, and will
Rise up
To end the madness of the bad
Who never had a chance
Against our power
Our dance will liberate
Not at the gate
But now, here, in my life
Or I will die
An old man trying
Crying for the children
Who cannot cry

I am not alone
You are my home
Beirut, Paris, Baghdad
I hold your hands
To understand
We can and will end this

The drones that kiss our kids
The vests that caress our sisters
The knives that drive our dads
The bullets that blast our brothers
The gas that strangles mothers
Of every religion or none
You are not alone
And in our joining
We are not alone too
We are you

The poetry of tax

There is no poetry in tax, you say
Then have you read Part IVA?
An easy task for tax men like me
But something else to set you free

You cannot avoid it, so it is said
Perhaps, unlike the dead,
It haunts us, taunts us, every day

It just will not go away
Grabs us at every pay
Takes our share of spending
Its grasp is never-ending

Except for the rich
Their Cayman Islands stitch
Means no tax here
Nothing to fear

For them, always them
We cannot end, pro tem
Or avoid their capital
All hail, these avoiders

The swank rank rich
Whose laws we hitch
To loins ungirded
Herded past the paying point

It is their joint
The house on the point
You can feel the sea
Not you, not me

And the pin-suit brigade
Scream 'well played'
And judges nod oh so wise
What a clever tax devise

They travel on our roads
Clog hospitals with loads
Make money off our schools
We are their educated fools

Our taxes in their slackness
Build their non-taxes, our laxness
Pays their lives, a blackness
That survives our best

They miss the rack
We pay our tax
And all the untaxed rest
Is our wealth, blessed

In their hands, no lands
And no place to pay
Homage to the altar
Of profit, no falter

In pursuit, they win
Again
Is there no end
To their wending?

No happy ending
No paying tax
Only the usual
The whacks for us

My hand stretches out
The man with clout
Takes his tithe
I am, just, alive

He thrives
I exist
That is the cyst
Their system of untax

The poetry is but a tale
Of tax for us
And not for them
This must end

But when, but when?
And in the distance
The super yachts glisten
Golden in the sand and groves

We live on loaves
Of week old bread
They live on labour, dead
And alive

While we arrive
For work, again
And paying taxes
Till our end

While they live on
And on and on
Doing no wrong
And paying no tax

It is their road
Built by our labour
Not their money
In their safe harbour

Their tax is an option
Their games Olympian
Their laws gargantuan
And us, we pay

In every way
Our payment is our blood
No flood of tears from them
Only smug delight

They have done it right
And we bear the cost
It is their win
It is our loss

Unread

I shall walk among the books
And gather half remembered looks
From people
Who no longer care
And dance around their airs and graces
Of forgotten fortune in other places
Until the folio of pages becomes our ages
That fevered, face their rages
And calm the beast
Not least, alone, horn shorn
And grown wise in others' eyes
Where plants are seeded
In love that spreads its needs
And bleeds, all bleeding
For the needing and the loss
This is the way the books will stay
Remain, in pain
Like us, unread

Morning comes early

Morning comes early
Not in glory
But revenge
Edge, edging closer
To the edge
Its trumpet blast
Shakes awake
The dead
As so begins, again,
The same
The trudge trudge trudge
Of each name
In the grudge, grudge, grudge
Of fighting
Sunlight
To gain
The right
To live, renewed

We have reviewed
The past all night
Refreshed
On memories
Of delight
Or fright
So stale
We do not fail
But fall
Back
To open eyes

And surprise ourselves
In the built dark shelves
Of life
Where twins the wife
Of everyman
Handy in the glad
Handling in the mad
And no more taken
Than the sad
Morning
That has come
Early
Embrace, the enemy

For a friend, again

You think
No, there is none
No everlasting,
No fun

We think
Not true
We begin with you
Again, and again

You think
To run from or to?
Is that you? Or me?
Could it be,
Your ecstasy,
All agony?

We know
The reins are taken
The horse, mistaken
And all the while
The child
Plays their own

Not grown but growing
To the land of less
Knowing
And in its decline
Pass the wine!

That should help
And keep dry
Our place from why
And where
Who cares?

We do
We love you
My friend
Let this begin
Not end

You are our friend
We yours too
It is time, to renew
Our bonds
Live long
Together

On the sewer we sup

The old man sits in New York
Every word, every squawk
Rattles their power
In his fifty year hour

And while he sits
His empire shits the news
A world of blues
And little hope

We are our dopes
Caught for the times
Of hope, today
The sun rises, away

There is no shine
Only New York whine
Where word is law
And his law is lord
A wink, a nod
Grab his rod!
A headline changed
Deranged, upon deranged

The sensible are now the mad
We have been had
Roll up, roll up
On the sewer we sup

The cricket crowd

Old men at the cricket
Are alike
Grey hair and beer bellies
Compete for sameness
Amongst the bald
While they walk in mumbles
And cuss their usness
The world is not
What they want
All gone, grown young
While they age
The clouds pass by
Beyond their rage

The cricket crowd wanders by
Meandering on alcohol's high
Arriving from retiree town
The old men frown
And women remain,
Always the same,
The other of desire,
The young men hire
Beer's fleeting pastime

The young women laugh, and wine
While older women shake their head
And children stand
Bats in hand
For the heroes to come
They run, and run
For signings on the day

Blind cricketers see us through
Their hit and miss is kissed
In love we watch
My friend, he bowls
The ball howls
We hear the game
It is the same

The chips and grog flow by
The ball ascends the sky
Polite applause greets us
The cause is just and right
As the lights
Fight the night
And the cold creates a blanket field
One side must yield
And does

The early end we fear
Caught between the old and near
We leave the pitch
The summer itch has begun
We want more fun, now
And this is how

Do not play cricket with my soul

Do not play cricket with my soul
On the seeming pitch of caught and bold
Where singles run from all despair
And bats are raised in the air
Where both ends run life's retreat
Amid soft declarations of defeat

The outfield is a gathering loss
Who braves the winning of the toss
And in the stands sits padded man
To slow the tide of their command
While ever slow the crowd it claps
Run out again for their mishaps

The bouncing ball catches fame
So much greater than just a game
Immortals reborn, immortals die
Will Bradman field me in the sky?
There is of course another hope
To see the cherry in the rope

The white man's ashes match his clothes
While the seagull creams its furry nose
The team belongs to none, at home,
We are all, yet all alone
With our voices raised in support
The scoreboard reads caught for nought

The sun is out here as well
But who can tell in this hell
For runs without tickets?
They chase our every wicket
While we foxtrot boycotts
That are out but are not

This is our life to stay in
For as long as the swing
Does not catch us out
Or the benefit of doubt
Gather our gloves to crease
With such ease we are deceased

And the innings is over
We applaud the plucky cover
Driver of sweet pretence
Into the picket fence
Of yesteryear so clear
The end is near, is here

All out we shout
There was no doubt
All out we cry
With one dry eye
The opening of your fun
Your innings has begun

Farewell, old man

The sea is blue
And I see you
Old man
Smiling in the waves
Waving
Drowning too
Your time is near
Embrace the fear
We will build
What you began

I cannot rescue you
Old man
You are beyond that
The sea is flat
And your drowning
Is deserved
The earth will live
That is what you give

Built today
On this we build
To save the dead, the killed
From your drowning arms
Your charms
It is your time to go
And ours to be born

We will not mourn
Your passing
Grasping for air

We do not care
We are on our land
In command

A new world is born
Torn from your hand
Your cold, lifeless, hand
We are born again
My friend

Our beginning is your end
Die happy
Knowing we will be
Free, at least, free
On your foundations
Solid as rocks
Taking stock

This is our way
Goodbye today
And thanks
Thanks for the base
We will use it
With taste
And have inscribed
On our banners
All manner of thing
The wages of sin
And abolition
From this position
That is where we begin
Farewell, old man

Citizen

Why do you ask
Citizen 973822001?
Surely the mandate is fun?
If not, we must talk
I can walk to your place

I am there already
I am the funny face
At the door
No need to knock me, nor
Mock me

My knock knees are free
As you will be
Soon, very soon
In our jails of freedom
You cannot beat 'em!

Monochrome world of liberty
March in line self sovereignty
Come join the party pleasure
There, that is the measure
Of all worth

This place, this earth
Is yours,
It is our cause, too
Why do you ask, Citizen 973822002?

Open libraries

The libraries are open
Because our minds are not
The books are free
Because we are not

This dialectic is the freedom current
Electric, electrifying
Terrifying and defying logic
So let me read to you

And through this
We can see the haze
And gather, razed,
Our razored senses

Close the libraries
and price the books
Is that what it took
For liberation?
Not in the knowledge nation
Where Orwell lives
And justice gives
Its name to what is and is not

Books are what we've got
And ideas, and actions too
That are open libraries
For our unfolding minds
For me, and for you

These broken waters of the truth

The words are there
You can hear them
Unborn but coming
These broken waters of the truth
Arrive too soon

The tears certainly are here
From Ankara to Nauru
And Aleppo
They flow everywhere
And grow each day
There is another way

The words
Parched parchment heard
Token, even absurd
Woken, aroused
By writing
And others' actions
Uniting our factions
And fight, not flight

The night is quiet
The cloak of death
Does that

And the tap, tap, tap, of the keyboard
Revives the way, forward,
Breaking the silence
Taking licence with truth
To make a verity
That helps, fleetingly
To set us free
In our minds
Now for our lives

Come, join our cause

We have only stones to throw
And shoes
What about you?

You have tanks, and guns, and armies
That leave us occupied
And by your side

You have the button,
The ultimate solution,
Perhaps, for us?

While your uncle curses,
His pocket money
Lines your purse

The worst is upon us still
Your hearse departs, unfilled,
With our bodies only

You cannot kill us all
We stand,
Sometimes we fall

And throw our stones
And shoes
You lose

You cannot win
You kill us
And we return

Your phosphorus can burn
So too our hearts
We yearn

For places
Grandparents knew
Before you, yes you,

Drove us
From our land
Terror in your hand

It will not destroy us
Or our love
For above all else

We will be free
One day,
One day

Our stones and shoes will free us
From the nightmare
The road to Cairo too

Is the way to Jerusalem
Not new, not old,
But bold

And ours, and yours,
Our freedom is yours
Come, join our cause

Our death is your death
Our life yours
Come, join our cause

One day too
You will be throwing
Stones and shoes

With us then
You will be free
And so shall we

We hear your thunders

We can hear you here
Your shouts of fear
And hope, keep shouting
Until the need to shout
Disappears

We will join you here
In your cries
Against their lies
And concentration camps
We will

We do not suffer
The same pain
Pain
We shout, again

Till we have no voice
And you have choice
That is not today
Nor in sorrow, tomorrow,
But the day after
We will hear your laughter

Your raped body
Your slit wrists
Your forced kissed mouth
Your broken bones
These are the heritage of hate

That the prison guards of profit
Here and there, promulgate
We are the prisoners
Of their fate, and ours

In the lonely hours
Before the dawn
That civilisation proclaims
We know your names
Not numbers
We hear your thunders

In the grave of no

We had long nights in common
Separate days our sentence
It was the sweet entrance I found in you
To love's physicality
And the pleasure of the two for me
That doomed us, roomed alone,
I rushed too quick from your throne

I remember the night
Every day
There was another way
A lifetime cannot change
The choice I made
And I have lost
Not just my voice
But the moist that was your touch
No more, enough

I am not tough
Your memory unfrees me
My memory denies me, freedom
I avoid the beaten
With these thoughts
It comes to naught
For an old man caught
In yesterday
There is another way

If you read this
Will you know it is you?
If I write this
Will I know it is me?
You do not read my words
For it was me who buried you
In the grave of no
There is no risen again

My never forgotten, my friend
Is this our final, the end
Of what could have been
The dream
Farewell, love's hell?

This is our final, the end
Of what could have been
The dream
Farewell, love's hell!

Lenin's anvil is worn

Lenin's anvil is worn
The hammering has torn
The new day, and shorn away,
Hope built upon
A vision, from yesterday

Trotsky's pen is dead
Stalin silenced,
Picked head
Where thoughts remain
Unlicensed, unread

We are the wrong
To right the long injustice
Of the past
For the future
And for us

No one can see
You or me
Are cursed free
While their freedom reins
To calm our chains

Our birthing pains began
A long hard labour
Stillborn, remains,
Do not mourn
Return the favour

Each child is ours
To love, to house
And to try, again
Our oath, my friends
This is our cry

We will rise
And rise, and rise
And only then
The anvil will renew
And the pen rewrite

Our plight is not
Servitude, or poverty
It is the quest
To be free
One day, one day

I can no more

I can no more write
Than I can breathe
With gaps and wheeze

My life is asthma puffs
And deluded enoughs
Where catch the breath
Is saved from death
Deep beneath the depth

Breathing, sleep awakes
And snakes a way
Catching others play
And throwing ball
We fall for nothing
But the past

And the last, last breath
Is coming quick
No fix, no future
Beyond all gone
I see the wrong
And right, myself

Too tight for help
Too old for joy
Except within
His grin is mine
I am that boy
So grand to stand
With him, and you

You all are me
We all are true
Banners of our lives

Conspire to hew away
The statue, yesterday,
The air is come
We are run
Rushed faces done
None, there is none
But ourselves

Together march and marched
Forever love and loved
We stay, with them
They stay, with us
The common oxygen
Of life and when
Is freedom come, again

Never, that's a word
I have not heard
Till the men in suits
Root roots and leave
Legacies of loots
That thieve the future
Our to come
Is gone

Reclaim it now
From the pirates,
Profits high
Tanks dry

I can no more breath
Than I can write
Under their rule
That is our plight
To fight, always, to fight

Monday is the time of silence

Monday is the time of silence
When all the doors are closed
When hooded men hunchback the streets
And the petty boys are nosed

This is the land where talk commands
A febrile passing glance
And strangers kiss in open fields
To meet again in dance

This is the place where echoes lace
The spirit of the mind
Where looks askance are saving grace
And kids are lost to find

So take the quiet in the crowd
And shout its name, loud and loud
The deaf can hear, the blind can see
The world is this totality

Gather not the shoes of poor rich men
But ask the question and answer when
The moneyed ones are ever jailed
If that is all then we have failed

I see the sandman very near
The Corban blessed, lighting fear
In hardened hearts near streets and walls
Glutted bulls win their falls

Monday is no longer silenced
Its rages burst their cone
Unveiling torment's terrible truth
We are many, they are alone

Who carries the carrion?

Who carries the carrion from conception to its death?

Who walks the smalling mile in slowly steepling steps?

We do not know my answers to questions we don't feel

Nor do we know the freedom of what is cruelly real

And yet we sense a truth that no one else can touch

For hope is not eternal, springing from our guts

It is the nuts and bolts of love, and life

Caught between the farmer, husband, wife

And who can say the other is the one for every day

And who can say the other needs be sent away?

Island bound, bound, gagged our humanity

Are we there yet they cry, to be free

I see the walking corpse of government made flesh

My retching flecks its body, building sweet distress

There go the youngest memories of David's shining Star

Our yellowing history pages calling from afar

But we are deaf to their past and our today

We turn our hearing down and our glance away

The soft sofa life together shouts leave us now,

Till our door knocks like those we cheered before

And the locks are gone like those we clapped to their shore

We are carrying the carrion that consigns us to our death

We will fight furiously their disease, to our lasting breath

Where are our words, today?

Have you been the morning, mourning?
Taken flight in night, and song?
Gathering, garnering the too long day…
To away with all?
And so to fall, to fall
For their catch cry, the call
The sweet absurd,
Caught in the ballad
Of their birds
Without our words
There is no way
Where are our words today?

October is coming

October is coming
Rushing through the decades
Our century bleeds its name
And we wait, the patient ones
Impatient in our turns
It burns, it burns
Our thoughts
Untaught ideas
Learned from streets
And books that took their time
To write
After October's truth

One hundred years of waiting
Still, quiet, still, riot
Still, waiting
No more, we call
We of the small groups
A minority that swoops
And wings its way
All the way
To today
And the land of not doing
Of not knowing

Like May, that will change
Like February, it will begin
Can we, will we win?
The old mole is grubbing well
Our heaven, their hell
Awaits, it waits
And baits the future
Breathing lessons
In and out
There is no doubt
October is coming

Still free

I walk with the dog every day
Past the dam of sunken dreams
The ducks were there today
With six children in tow
Four shepherds protecting them
From dogs and men,
And other predators

They are safe from us
As they glide the water
To their distance
The ripples ride the surface
And reach us on foreign shores
The other side of nowhere
In the midst of city

The golf course is pretty
Manufactured, hand groomed
With no one on it today
No one to play their course
In life and death,
He stops and I draw breath
In the bowel pause of walking

The flies are light
Unlike the paddocks nearby
But the heat remains
Even in the morning
Is this a warning?
I shrug and our rhythm returns
He earns another piss

A woman walks by close
We nod the strangers' nod
And grunt hellos
To those we do not know
The dog is unconcerned
Other than with smells
And shrub branches
To massage his back

Their shade is black
On the ground
Relief, but, what is this?
His mouth is full, again
Of things I wish unfound
He will survive
Another poo might do

Then the stopping stops
And the air sucking starts
In both our bodies and our hearts
Too soon the door attracts us
Attacks us
And his water is my tea
Another day, still free

To a tree

I cannot cut you down
For many years
You shaded me
And still do
You bought me joy
And still do
Your sight is soothing
You protect us all

I breathe you
And you me
I need you
Sweet tree
I cannot free you
From your roots
This earth gave birth
To you, and me

Death is not setting free
I cannot kill you
For cheaper energy
The panel has decided
You will live

And the sun can make its own way
Past the shadows of the past
You live
You are free, free at last

What gives me the right to decide?
Your fate is not mine to make
Or should not be
I invaded your land, not you mine
Rest easy my friend
I am but a carer
I give you to the children
To love

The butcher reigns

The butcher sharpens his knife
On the bones of his dead
While his Russian wife
Carves the cities
Of the children,
Bleeding, slowly bled

Big brother butcher
Sidelined, with no power
Cannot stop the slaughter
Caught in the moment
Taut in the hour

His daughter is near
She inspects the scene
Her long tress of bombs
Remain quiet and unseen

The fleeing die in camps,
Concentrating the mind
The children die in waves
The men are left behind

Freedom flags its name
And loses,
The game is over
For now
The butcher reigns

The once a year of cheer

The loneliness does not disappear
It grows, with Christmas
It cheers its way into homes
It sleighs askew the old
The new it leaves to you

While the homeless streets
Beg indifference to their needs
Who shares the bleeding?
Staunch defenders of today
There is no other way
Is hammered brain to brain

Without pain where is the again
Of yesteryear?
And depression
The fascist armies march
In step, side by bloody step
Until we are left
Without a left

Bereft, alone
Welcome home
For Christmas comes
The once a year of cheer
That isn't
Of beer that is

And escapes that aren't
An uncle's taunt
Haunts the fall
That is us all

When will the together gather?
The question that has no answer
Answers the answer
That has no question

Not never
But not now
Christmas is not here
Yet, and yet
It is close

In today tomorrow rises
Surprises all
The fall becomes the rising
Up beyond ourselves
Humanity is our saviour
Savouring self

Community calls
Deck the halls
With togethered dance
Take the chance

And grasp the new year
The new
Society for all
Not the few

Raise our glasses
Get off our arses
To our freedom
Ring in the day
Ring in the night
Fight, fight and fight

I can smell their hell
But know this
Under every mistletoe kiss
Liberation lies near
Christmas all the year
Is close

The old is closing
Down it goes
They do not know
Tomorrow waits
And their gates, unbending
Bend
I see the end
If not the ending

Do not lose sight
The night star
Is near
I can hear its light
Tomorrow is Christmas
Every day

Never sway from that
Goal and bell this fact
Our future is you, and me
Now

Join hands around the pyre
Of hate
Stop the sewer of contemplaters
Right thinking men

Token women in their crew
Nothing is new
Except what we make
Today but our work
And shall unmake our work
Tiresome, dreary
Into love

And reclaim ourselves
All ourselves
Let's celebrate
The darkness is late
The flame approaches
Embrace the light

And gift the future to today
The only way
Freedom is near
I can hear her call
Embrace this
And with that rejoice
Find our voice

And yell from the treetops
Stop! The old ways are dead
My head is clear now
I can see from on high
I know why

And so do you
Let's join anew
The battle for a better world
Heaven here
Not afar
Is what we will make
It is ours to take

Sing with me in the rain

I shall stand in the rain
And yell at the clouds
Loudly, aloud
Allowed in old age
The place where rage
Grows and knows,
Knows what?

Not much
Hence the rage
And writing on a page
The words of anger
Of danger that haunts
Our meaning
Meaningless
There is no feeling
No kiss

That is this
And still it rains
Will the government do nothing?
But that is the point
Of this government
Of terrorists and boats
There is no hope
But the proles

I grow old
My short trousers roll
Over my tummy
Not funny
Another's reasoned rage
And mine too

And now the sun has cooled
Making fools of us
Nothing but the plus
Added to our knowledge
I will retire
And tax my writing
In a land where the rain
Speaks French

Or where steel men
Turn coke around
And the old man falls
Without telling me
The shouting stops
We will be free
Of bitterness

Maintain our rage
In our age
The age of anger
Needed anger
Against a world so wrong
I will sing my songs
Against and for
Sing with me
Sing with me
In the rain

Waiting for May

Soyez réalistes, demandez l'impossible

I wait for May
Like a dream
So far away
And 68ers gather
Remembering
Times past
It did not last

I was a child man
Of school and maths
And Vietnam
Impending drafts awoke me
Paris provoked me

Now I am a grown child man
The fire of the streets
And factories
Burns still
Overshadows the hill

And its poor light
And memories recount
The loss we had
In sight behind
The fight
We did not join
They did not know!

And now I know
The impossible is our need
Today
Not the plod plod plodding
Of that day
But '*De l'audace, encore de l'audace, et toujours de l'audace*'
There is no other way

www.ingramcontent.com/pod-product-compliance
Lightning Source LLC
Chambersburg PA
CBHW070924080526
44589CB00013B/1420